THE IMPERISHABLE SUPREME

(BASED ON BHAGAVAD GITA CHAPTER-8)

DR. JAGADEESH PILLAI

Contents

Paryer

HARE RAMA HARE RAMA, RAMA RAMA HARE HARE
- HARE KRISHNA, HARE KRISHNA, KRISHNA
KRISHNA, HARE HARE

(Mantra - Kali Santaranopanishad)

Dedication

|| DEDICATED TO THE IMPRISHABLE SUPREME ITSELF ||

About The Author

Dr. Jagadeesh Pillai a voracious reader, Four Times Guinness World Record holder, writer, and true research scholar was born in Varanasi, the abode of Lord Shiva. He is Ph.D. in Vedic Science. He is a multi-faceted polymath with innate qualities, creative ideas and many remarkable achievements. Although his roots extend back to "Gods own Country"(Kerala), the residents of Varanasi feel proud of him and adore him as a child of Varanasi who caters to every individual in need without any expectations. A deep study into his profile reflects that he has added so many feathers to his cap which makes him quite unique. He is a four times Guinness Book of World Records Holder in the following subjects :

"Script to Screen" which he achieved by producing and directing a state of art animation film within the shortest time possible by breaking the earlier set record by Canadians. There are many national and international Awards and Recognitions to his credit.

Longest Line of Post Cards which he has done on the occasion of 163 years of Indian Postal Day by 16300 post cards. The event was also connected with a questionnaire about Indian Flag.

Largest Poster Awareness Campaign – This was achieved by designing an awareness campaign on the subject "Beti Bachao – Beti Padhao".

Largest Envelop – Towards tribute to Prime Minister's initiative 'Make in India' – he has created about 4000 sq meter envelop using waste papers.

Attempted by lighting 70000 candles on a 210 kg cake to celebrate the 70th Indian Independence day recorded in World Records India.

Attempted a documentary on Dhamek Stupa of Sarnath dubbing in 17 languages, result is waiting from Guinness World Records.

He is versatile in Gita teaching. The young generation is fond of his Gita teaching and he has changed the life of many young through his continued motivational boost up and teachings.

He has composed and sung Gayatri Mantra in 1000 different tunes.

He has composed and sung Hanuman Chalisa in 108 different tunes.

He has composed and sung hundreds of Sanskrit Bhajans, Patriotic songs, etc.

He has written and directed so many short films and documentaries for awareness campaigns.

He has done voluntary services to UP Police and Kerala Police to spread awareness campaigns on the various issue through videos and photography.

He is on the path of authoring thousands of books on Indian culture, Indian Temples, and the life of extraordinary people.

It is hard to believe that he has produced and directed more than 100 Documentaries on a particular city (Varanasi) which is done by a single person.

He has helped and guided more than 25 boys and girls to achieve world records through various creative and innovative methods.

A multifaceted person who can apply the best of his intellect using the God-given blessings which have been showered upon every human being granting them an immense capacity to learn, experience, and experiment with many things and do wonders in this world of discrimination and disparities.

He is a teacher and a student at the same time who always learns every day and teaches every day. As a master, his weakness was that he never sticks to a particular subject. Perhaps this weakness gives him the strength to master any area which he came across.

Each of his days dawned with learning a new topic and he spend most of his time experimenting and researching it.

He is also a selfless social activist and a motivational speaker.

His life was full of struggle, ups and downs, and failures. But he never gave up and faced all his trials and tribulations full of confidence. Today he is a successful young man with a lot of enthusiasm and rich life experience.

He has sung full Ram Charita Manas 51 hours audio by his own composition. He has also sung the whole Bhagavad-Gita in his own composition with a rhythmic background.

He has also sung "Lokah Samastha Sukhino Bhavantu" in 50 different languages.

Currently working on a detailed and scientific study on Veda, Upanishad, Puranas, Bhagavad Gita, etc.

Currently, he is the Hon' Chancellor of 'Eurasia Digital University'.

Awards

Four Times Guinness World Records

Winner of Mahatma Gandhi Vishwa Shanti Puraskar

Mahatma Gandhi Global Peace Ambassador
Kashi Ratna Award

Dr. APJ Abdul Kalam Motivational Person of the Year 2017

Mother Teresa Award

Indira Gandhi Priyadarshini Award

Bharat Vikas Ratna Award

Udyog Ratna Award

Vigyan Prasar Award

Poorvanchal Ratn Samman

Preface

The wise scholars who has achieved the wisdom and intelligence, direct connection with the Supreme and always does every action towards dedication to the Supreme gets the same status and quality as the Supreme. He can expand him limitlessly and do wonders in the world for the benefit/inspiration of all being.

The Soul can get a status like the Sun which spreads its light and energy equally to everything on the earth towards its obligatory duty to the Supreme.

The secrets and power of Imperishable Supreme are explained in this book in a simple language connected with day to day life.

THE IMPERISHABLE SUPREME

In the end of the seventh chapter of Bhagavad Gita, Krishna has mentioned few words/names without explaining about it. Out of curiosity, Arjuna has asked Krishna to explain about it.

The Words/Names are :

Brahman

Adyatmam

Karmam

Adhibhootam

Adhidaivam

Actually the totality of all the above is the whole Universe.

Lets try to understand it :

BRAHMAN

The Supreme, the ultimate Authority, the creator of everything.

ADYATMAM

Means Spirituality

(nature of Supreme and its actions like Karma Sanyasi).

Does everything, did nothing. Vishnu Form. All are equally treated under one umbrella, no any kind of discrimination, no punishment, no boons, no credit or fruit expectation, flawless

KARMAM

All kinds of Actions done by the creations of nature

Seed sprouting, water evaporation, raining, fruits in the trees, all actions of birds, all actions of animals, all actions of all other specieis, even the action of an atom rotation within it, all the actions of human (speaking, listening, seeing, touching, smelling, etc. etc.)

ADHIBHOOTAM

Perishable part of every creation like human body, body of various other birds, animals, wood, leaf, etc.

ADHIDAIVAM

Divinity (chetana) within every creation. The Soul as a part and particle of the Supreme in every creation. Because the Soul a body of a human or any other species activates, if the soul and its divinity is not there, the body will be called as "dead body - adhibhootam"

ADHIYAGYAN

We have already discussed about various "sacrifices" in previous chapters. Every action (karma) is included with "an intention" plus "sacrifice" and the "fruit" of it.

Intention+Sacrifice+Fruit = Karma (action)

An example of Sacrifice by human :

Action:

Planted a Tree

Intention of action:

Selfless, more oxygen, fruit, vitamins, etc. for the

generation to come.

Sacrifice:

time, money, ego (selfish)

Fruit of Action:

Oxygen, fruits of tree, shadow, vitamins for others and _generating good karma for self and destroying bad karma_

An example of Sacrifice by the Supreme :

In the above action of human, this action and sacrifice of _"generating good karma and destroying bad karma"_ is automatically happens without the involvement of human. A human cannot calculate how much good karma generated or how much bad karma generated.

Another example is : when the Soul leave the body (body is sacrificed), destroyed and merged with five elements and and all the atoms get disintegrated to come back to its original form.

Like the above there are various other actions and sacrifices are happening in the body of creations and in the nature also and the the Supreme is the only authority who does such sacrifices.

That is why the Supreme is also called "Adhi-Yagyan", based on the various sacrifices done by it.

There is a word **"ADHIKARI"** in sanskrit/hindi which means "the Authority". So in the above _Adhi-bhootam_ means the authority of perishable particles, _Adhi-Daivam_ means the authority of divine particles and the _Adhi-Yagyan_ means the authority of divine sacrifies. (1-4/8).

***

What about the state of mind at the time of death?

The wise scholars who has achieved the wisdom and intelligence, direct connection with the Supreme and always does every action towards dedication to the Supreme gets the same status and quality as the Supreme. He can expand him limitlessly and do wonders in the world for the benefit/inspiration of all being.

Means, the Soul can get a status like the Sun which spreads its light and energy equally to everything on the earth towards its obligatory duty to the Supreme, (like an employee becomes Boss of the company). (5/8).

For example we can think about the people like Dr. APJ Abdul Kalam, Swami Vivekananda, Ramana Maharshi, etc. There are thousands of such people on the earth. We will know them by their wisdom, selfless action and sacrifices, not through publicity. They achieves the state of "Aham-Brahmasmi", "I am alike the Supreme".

When they have achieved a completely purified mind which is free from desires and free from attachments with any kind of worldly pleasures, physical and material things, then what they will do on the earth. Either they will do some big things in the world using their intelligence for the benefit of the world (like Dr. APJ Abdul Kalam) or teach/share people (like Swami Vivekananda/Ramana Maharshi) how to achieve the ultimate quality/status as the Supreme to do selfless actions for the benefit all.

***

So every human has to try to establish a direct connection with the Supreme. Face all the situations of life by dedicating its fruits even if it is a tension, stress, pain, desire, etc. to the Supreme. Through continues practise and concentration we can achieve the purity of mind and a purified mind directly connects to the Supreme. While doing every action, just feel that we are an instrument of

God.

For some people it will take many births to understand and achieve the wisdom and intelligence about the Supreme. It can be achieved either through a wisdom achieved scholar or it will automatically happen when we practise by fixing our mind to the Supreme while doing every action.

Shri Buddha got the realisation when he saw a deadbody. Shri Shankarachary got it when a low born out caste person realises him about the importance and differentiation between soul and body, Maharshi Valmiki got it from Naradji and turned from Ratnakar to Valmiki Maharshi. (7-8/8).

***

Through daily practise, with a balanced purified mind, we can fix our concentration between the eyebrows and meditate upon the Supreme with the understanding that the Supreme is like the smaller than the smallest particle atom, but spread everywhere and the ultimate authority of all. Those who continue the practise, will achieve the state/status as the Supreme even at the time of death. (9-10/8).

***

Our actions and the fear of death

We does such millions of actions from childhood to old age, but it is not possible to recall what we did each day. We can hardly recall only very few important ones or the very recent actions. The same way, we forgot all the actions what we did in our past birth also.

At the time of death, we try to recall various actions we did in our past and our mind has stuck to few of those most interested ones. (may be about properties, children, business, etc.). His next birth will also be same per his interest and thoughts at the time of death like we planned something last night and did the same in the morning. But the death is automatically an inbuilt/embedded truth with every birth, but we forgot it.

That's why it is said that, the purity of mind happens, when your mind is fully filled with goodness. If there is a mad person with an ugly look resides near by you and whenever you see him, your mind fills with anger, hatred and abuse him and the whole day or very often you are happily discuss about his madness, ugli look, attitude and habits to various people and that time all those dirts are doubles and stores in your mind. Whenever you think about him, his face will come in your imagination and his ugliness will come as abuse in your speech. But nothing happens to the madman because of your imagination, thoughts and words about him, but your mind become impure and the whole dirt of him is stored in your mind like a waste dirty garbbage.

We should intelligently think and to keep the mind clean from all those unwanted thoughts.

If you don't like alcohol and the person who takes alcohol, then you never ever think about alcohol, discuss about it and him.

You becomes great and great depending the purity of your mind and the purity of your mind depends the purity in your imagination, actions, thoughts and speech. This is called a person with developed culture.

Sometime we can see in temples that the devotee or priest cleans the deity, (Shivlinga, etc) multiple times with clean water, pure milk, sandel, fragrance etc. and later decorate it with various flowers. The look will be very attractive, eye catching and divine. We will then bend and salute the deity and pray for the blessings and to fulfil our desires.

But ultimately, the action done on the deity resembles the cleaning of our own Soul with mind and senses.

Will you be using dirty water, faded flowers, uncleaned milk, etc. to decorate the diety? No.

But we are ignorant about it. We also need to clean our mind and decorate the soul in the same as way we cleaned and decorated the deity.

When the purification and decoration of our Soul and Deity happens in the same way, the manifestation of goodness in our life happens.

***

If a person who did a lot of bad actions in the past came to know that in the next five days he will be leaving the world and when we later check his action of those five days, we can find that not a single bad action he has been done. The fear of death has changed his mind to do something good atleast for those five days. Whether we remember or not, but the truth of death will always remain with us wherever we go whatever we do. Somebody has well said that, "every breath of us taking us towards greaveyard". Whatever power, wealth, relations you have, all are invain when you are like an unhealthy, tired, weak deer in front of the lion of death.

There are few people who are very eager to do something good and selfless before death, but their health, intelligence, etc. will be very weak at that time. They will realise that the whole life spent on waste and selfish things, even worshipped God to fulfil their own desiers and never ever thought to do something to satisfy the God or the Supreme.

More methods to connect the Supreme directly.

Normally the people worship various God forms to fullfull their own desires, not to understand the Soul or to achieve the God status itself. Such people needed statue, photos, painting, etc. and also some expectations will be there behind their God worshipping.

But the Supreme is formless so no photos, statue, etc. and because of that nobody can worship the formless Supreme to achieve anything material except to achieve the Supreme itself.

Formless God worshipping is very difficult, so if a person is eager to start direct formless God worshipping they can concentrate and chant the mantra "Om", meditate on it instead of a statue or photo of God and this practise will connect to the Supreme directly.

The continues and daily practise of meditation on "OM" will help to gradually detach from various worldly physical and material involvement and help to achieve the state/status as the Supreme. Even if they gets a new birth, the same status will continue and that's why they will be able to expand the level of their life and do wonders in the world for the benefit of all. Practise of meditation, concentration, mind purification, etc. and direct connectivity with the Supreme helps to get permanent mental peace and satisfaction and thus develops our intelligence to a very higher level. They won't be free from the miserable life struggles. Struggle and unpeacefulness happens when we are running to fulfil various desires, but if our desires are limited just to meet our immediate necessity of living, then we can be peaceful and satisfactory in life.

We can see a lot of people who are born in a normall family with limited resources, but still they do wonders and expands the level of their living which is not possible for a person who has every resources.

Taking birth on the earth or not, both are equal for them. (11-16/8/).

***

There are two different periods in a year called Uttarayan & Dakshinayan.

Uttarayan Period – between January to June

Dakshinayan Period – between July to December

Uttarayan Period is considered as very auspicious period, more light on the earth like the flames of fire. Fire represent for action and sacrifice.

Fire will make us energetic and enthusiastic and the same fire will help us to sacrifice and clean the mental dirts.

This period is actually very auspicious for wisdom achievers. They can do more and more selfless actions and can reap more goodness. The energy of the earth will make them energetic and more intellectual to do various selfless actions enthusiastically. Their wisdom and intelligence will be at its peak.

This auspicious time period is very useful and a chance for the old aged persons also who is expecting death at anytime and has a keen desire to achieve the wisdom and understanding about the Supreme. He should atleast try to clean his mind with good thoughts, detaching from material desire and attachment, practise forgiveness and can chant divine names of God or OM etc. to concentrate and connect with the Supreme.

Atleast at the time of death, if he understood the reality of the Supreme & connects with Supreme and if by chance his death happens, he won't take any more birth on earth.

Those who achieves the same status as the Supreme , such soul can achieve any other position apart from human like a star or something else in the universe because the soul has the same power as the Supreme. The same soul can become a Sun or Human.

****

In the same way during the period of "Dakshinayan" if an old aged person of a wisdom seeker, is expecting death at any time, his feelings won't be that auspicious. He will feel more uncomfortable, painful, feeling dark everywhere, he will memories the dark part of action he did in his life. Since he already entered into wisdom seeking many of his bad karmas might have been cleaned. So if he by chance leaves the body, all the good karmas he earned wil remain and with that good karma, his Soul can stay near the moon till the good karma remains and after that comes back takes a new birth.

One should take atmost care while doing any action during this period because the effect of any wrong doings will high high effect and will generate a lot of bad karma.

***

All other ignorant people who are totally engaged in their own world of pleasures, attachment with physical and material things forgetting the Supreme, will continue the miserable and painful life of birth and death whether they leave the body in Uttarayan or Dakshinayan.

***

So the human who wish to qualify from Tamasik, Rajasik and Satvik gunas, will always try to do selfless karmas to achieve the level and status same as the Supreme.

***

An Important Note:

To keep the knowledge as simple as possible, easily understandable and useful to apply in our life, few unwanted informations are omitted to explain from this chapter. But those who are so curious to learn more secrets and knowledge about the Supreme, please read the Chandogyopanishad (atleast Chapter-4) and Brihadaranyopanishad (atleast Chapter-6) slowly, understanding the word to word meaning in detail.

English Text of Slokhas of Bhagavad Gita Chapter-8 for Quick Reference

1,2

arjuna uvācha
kiṁ tad brahma kim adhyātmaṁ kiṁ karma puruṣhottama
adhibhūtaṁ cha kiṁ proktam adhidaivaṁ kim uchyate
adhiyajñaḥ kathaṁ ko 'tra dehe 'smin madhusūdana
prayāṇa-kāle cha kathaṁ jñeyo 'si niyatātmabhiḥ

3

śhrī bhagavān uvācha
akṣharaṁ brahma paramaṁ svabhāvo 'dhyātmam uchyate
bhūta-bhāvodbhava-karo visargaḥ karma-sanjñitaḥ

4

adhibhūtaṁ kṣharo bhāvaḥ puruṣhaśh chādhidaivatam
adhiyajño 'ham evātra dehe deha-bhṛitāṁ vara

5

anta-kāle cha mām eva smaran muktvā kalevaram
yaḥ prayāti sa mad-bhāvaṁ yāti nāstyatra sanśhayaḥ

6

yam yam vāpi smaran bhāvam tyajatyante kalevaram
tam tam evaiti kaunteya sadā tad-bhāva-bhāvitaḥ

7

tasmāt sarveṣhu kāleṣhu mām anusmara yudhya cha
mayyarpita-mano-buddhir mām evaiṣhyasyasanśhayam

8

abhyāsa-yoga-yuktena chetasā nānya-gāminā
paramam puruṣham divyam yāti pārthānuchintayan

9, 10

kavim purāṇam anuśhāsitāram
aṇor aṇīyānsam anusmared yaḥ
sarvasya dhātāram achintya-rūpam
āditya-varṇam tamasaḥ parastāt
prayāṇa-kāle manasāchalena
bhaktyā yukto yoga-balena chaiva
bhruvor madhye prāṇam āveśhya samyak
sa tam param puruṣham upaiti divyam

11

yad akṣharam veda-vido vadanti
viśhanti yad yatayo vīta-rāgāḥ
yad ichchhanto brahmacharyam charanti
tat te padam saṅgraheṇa pravakṣhye

12

sarva-dvārāṇi sanyamya mano hṛidi nirudhya cha
mūrdhnyādhāyātmanaḥ prāṇam āsthito yoga-dhāraṇām

13

oṁ ityekākṣharaṁ brahma vyāharan mām anusmaran
yaḥ prayāti tyajan dehaṁ sa yāti paramāṁ gatim

14

ananya-chetāḥ satataṁ yo māṁ smarati nityaśhaḥ
tasyāhaṁ sulabhaḥ pārtha nitya-yuktasya yoginaḥ

15

mām upetya punar janma duḥkhālayam aśhāśhvatam
nāpnuvanti mahātmānaḥ sansiddhiṁ paramāṁ gatāḥ

16

ā-brahma-bhuvanāl lokāḥ punar āvartino 'rjuna
mām upetya tu kaunteya punar janma na vidyate

17

sahasra-yuga-paryantam ahar yad brahmaṇo viduḥ
rātriṁ yuga-sahasrāntāṁ te 'ho-rātra-vido janāḥ

18

avyaktād vyaktayaḥ sarvāḥ prabhavantyahar-āgame
rātryāgame pralīyante tatraivāvyakta-sanjñake

19

bhūta-grāmaḥ sa evāyaṁ bhūtvā bhūtvā pralīyate
rātryāgame 'vaśhaḥ pārtha prabhavatyahar-āgame

20

paras tasmāt tu bhāvo 'nyo 'vyakto 'vyaktāt sanātanaḥ
yaḥ sa sarveṣhu bhūteṣhu naśhyatsu na vinaśhyati

21

avyakto 'kṣhara ityuktas tam āhuḥ paramāṁ gatim
yaṁ prāpya na nivartante tad dhāma paramaṁ mama

22

puruṣhaḥ sa paraḥ pārtha bhaktyā labhyas tvananyayā
yasyāntaḥ-sthāni bhūtāni yena sarvam idaṁ tatam

23, 24, 25, 26

yatra kāle tvanāvṛittim āvṛittiṁ chaiva yoginaḥ
prayātā yānti taṁ kālaṁ vakṣhyāmi bharatarṣhabha
agnir jyotir ahaḥ śhuklaḥshaṇ-māsā uttarāyaṇam
tatra prayātā gachchhanti brahma brahma-vido janāḥ
dhūmo rātris tathā kṛiṣhṇaḥshaṇ-māsā dakṣhiṇāyanam
tatra chāndramasaṁ jyotir yogī prāpya nivartate
śhukla-kṛiṣhṇe gatī hyete jagataḥ śhāśhvate mate
ekayā yātyanāvṛittim anyayāvartate punaḥ

27

naite sṛitī pārtha jānan yogī muhyati kaśhchana
tasmāt sarveṣhu kāleṣhu yoga-yukto bhavārjuna

28

vedeṣhu yajñeṣhu tapaḥsu chaiva
dāneṣhu yat puṇya-phalaṁ pradiṣhṭam
atyeti tat sarvam idaṁ viditvā
yogī paraṁ sthānam upaiti chādyam

Contact

9839093003

myrichindia@gmail.com

facebook.com/drjagadeeshpillaiofficial

youtube.com/drjagadeeshpillai